A Monk named Jocelin
Life in an abbey in medieval England

NORMAN SCARFE

SERIES EDITOR : BRIAN CHAPLIN

CHAMBERS

1. Jocelin, his book, and the Angevin Empire

 To think about

1. Use a large-scale 'physical' map of Eastern England, and see how the stone for building Bury abbey could have been brought from the quarries of Barnack.

2. We know that a copy of Jocelin's Chronicle was made a hundred years after his time. The monks obviously thought that it was a useful book. Why was this?

 To find out

3. Copy the Angevin family-tree from page 4 on to the biggest sheet of paper you can get. Then try to find a picture of every person named on the tree, and add that to the diagram. These pictures could either be cut out of comics and magazines, or copied from other books.

 To do

4. Imagine you are one of the people of Bury listed in Domesday Book. Have a talk with one of your friends about these new French rulers, and then write down some of the things you have said.

5. Use the picture of Adam the Cellarer, and draw a similar one of Jocelin. Paste this on to a large sheet of paper. Then, around the picture, illustrate the various kinds of work that Jocelin had to do as cellarer. You will find these on page 8, and you may find some things you want to add when you read later chapters. Give a title to the whole sheet.

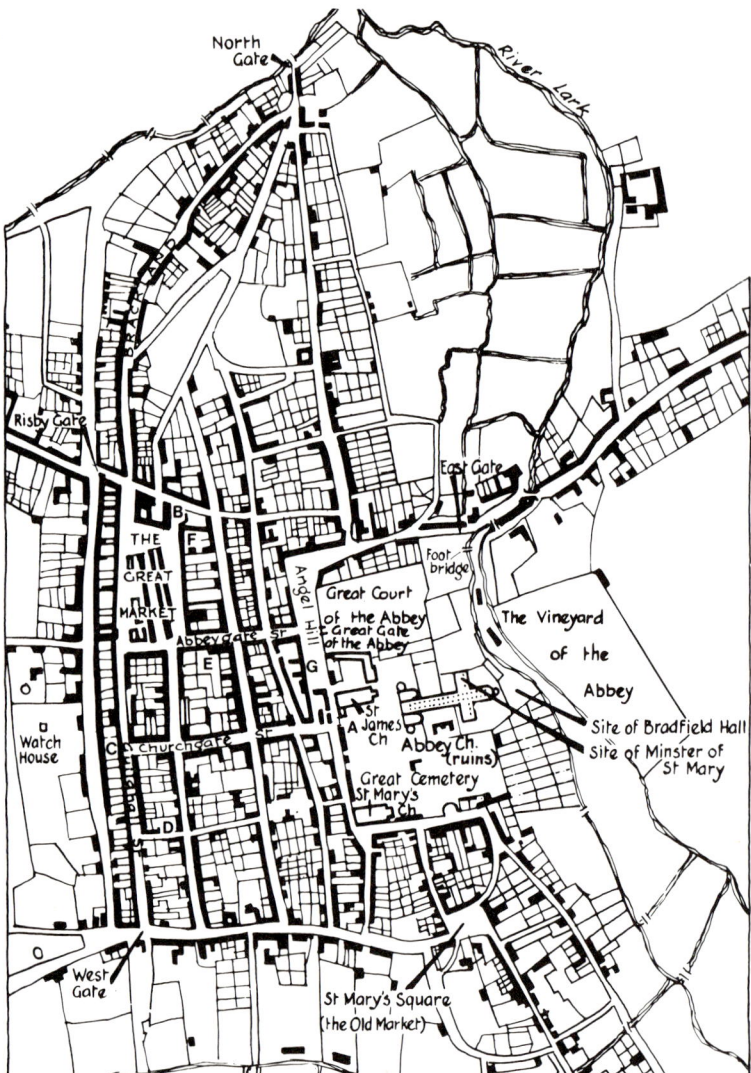

Jocelin's full name was Jocelin of Brakelond. This tells us that as a boy he lived in Brakelond, a newly-built corner of the town called Bury St Edmunds in south-east England. The name Brakelond meant 'broken land', land that was newly 'broken in'. A hundred years before Jocelin was born, William the Conqueror and his companions (who ruled Normandy, in France) took over England. They ruled from castles, mostly strongholds of timber set up on great round-topped earthworks. They easily took control of Bury, and needed no castle there, for a Frenchman had already been made abbot, the head of a big monastery, at Bury a whole year *before* the Norman Conquest in 1066.

A St James's 12th century steeple gateway leading to west front of abbey church

B Moyses Hall, 12th century

C,D Remains of Norman houses

E,F Possible Norman remains

G Angel Hotel, 13th century

Bury prospered from the very start of the new Norman rule. While other English towns resisted the Conqueror and were flattened, Bury expanded. In the photograph and plan on these pages, you can see the square grid lay-out of the planned Norman streets. You will find Brakelond, where Jocelin lived, in the top left-hand corner of the plan. It is now spelled 'Brackland'.

Bury was then a rich, bustling 'boom' town. Domesday Book described it (in Latin) like this:

'In 1086 the town covers a greater area than it did in 1066. It includes land that used then to be ploughed and sown, on which there are altogether 30 priests, deacons, and clergymen, 28 nuns and poor people who daily utter prayers for the king and all Christian people; altogether there are 75 millers, ale-brewers, tailors, washerwomen, shoemakers, robemakers, cooks, carriers and accountants. All these daily wait upon the Saint [that is, upon the abbey in which St Edmund's body was buried], and on the abbot and the brethren. Besides whom, 13 reeves [officials] over the land have their houses in the town, and under them 5 servants. Now there are 34 knights, French and English together, and under them 22 servants. There are now 342 houses on land that used to be under the plough.'

This sudden big increase in the number of houses shows us that the whole planned grid of streets must date from these twenty years between 1066 and 1086. We shall come back later to look at the details in the picture. One thing Domesday Book does not describe is St Edmund's abbey itself, which was also expanding and was the fourth richest abbey in England. The abbey's church was being rebuilt, with stone brought mostly by river from some famous English quarries at Barnack, near Stamford and Peterborough. On the plan on page 2, the great new abbey church is outlined in the shape of a cross. Work out for yourself where it stood (it is near the edge of the photo on page 3). When it was finished, in Jocelin's day, it was one of the biggest and most magnificent buildings in the whole world. Jocelin entered it as a 'novice', a new monk who had decided to learn to live and work in the monastery, in the year 1173. You can see a novice being accepted by some monks in the picture below.

When Jocelin joined St Edmund's abbey, Henry II was king, ruling England and most of France as you can see from the map opposite. *England* and *Normandy* came to Henry from his mother, Matilda, William the Conqueror's grand-daughter. Matilda's husband was Geoffrey of Anjou. People from Anjou are called Angevins, which explains why Henry II and his sons, Richard the Lionheart and John, are called the Angevin kings.

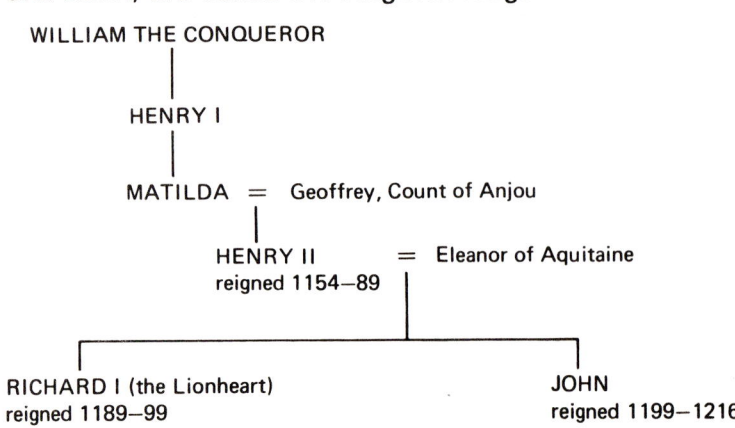

WILLIAM THE CONQUEROR

HENRY I

MATILDA = Geoffrey, Count of Anjou

HENRY II = Eleanor of Aquitaine
reigned 1154—89

RICHARD I (the Lionheart)
reigned 1189—99

JOHN
reigned 1199—1216

4

From his father, Henry came to have both *Anjou* and *Maine* (whose capital, Le Mans, is now most widely known as a motor-racing centre). *Brittany* Henry II inherited from his brother. Finally, Henry got *Aquitaine,* beautiful lands reaching down to the mountains of the Pyrenees, by marrying Eleanor of Aquitaine.

So Jocelin, and Bury, were part of a vast empire whose rulers spoke French and whose scholars spoke and wrote Latin. The English spoken then could not be understood by English-speaking people today. Our English is a mixture which includes a lot of that old French of Henry and his barons. It began to take its modern shape in the time of the poet Chaucer, two centuries after Jocelin.

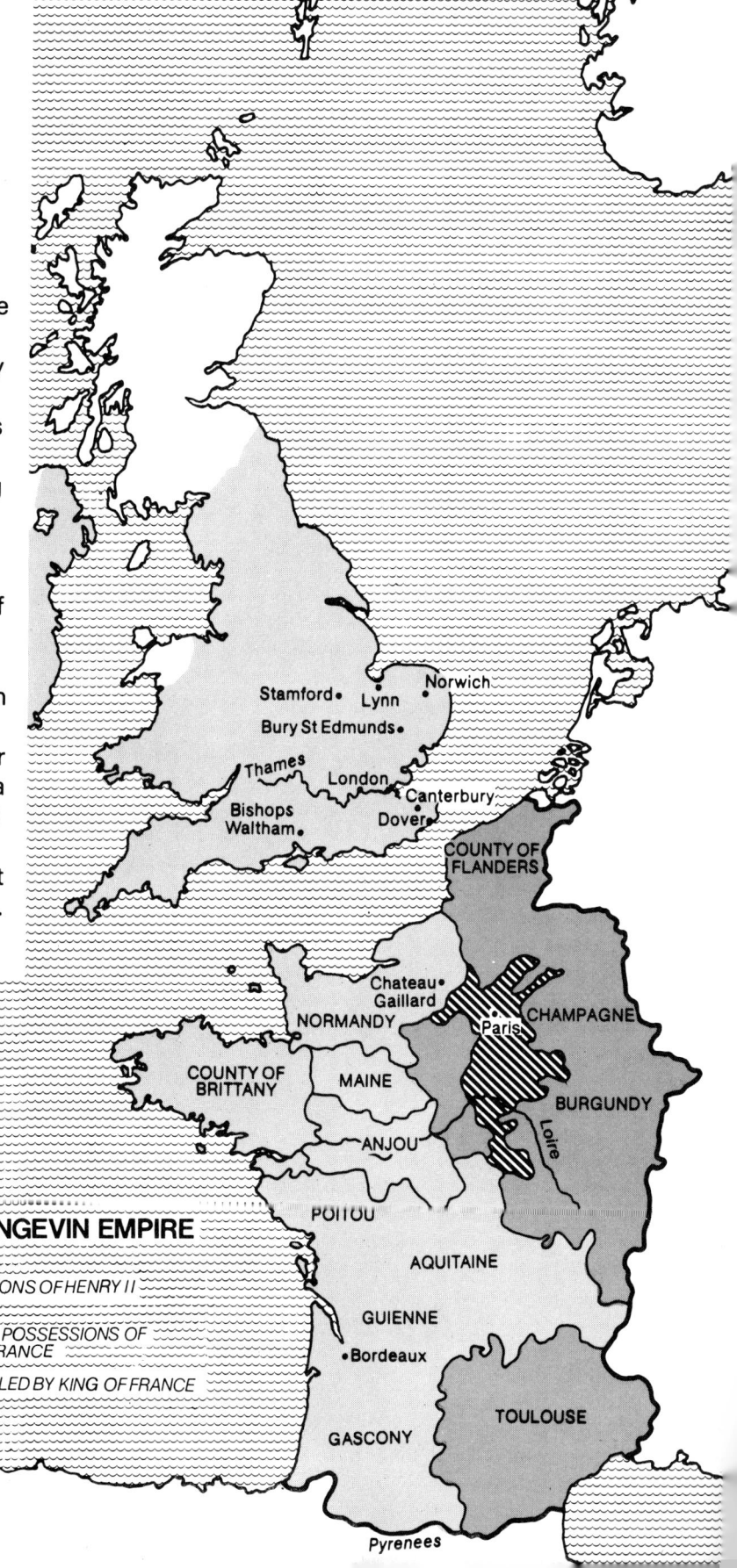

Stamford •   Lynn •   Norwich •

Bury St Edmunds •

Thames   London •

Bishops Waltham •

Canterbury •

Dover •

COUNTY OF FLANDERS

Chateau Gaillard •

NORMANDY

Paris

CHAMPAGNE

COUNTY OF BRITTANY

MAINE

ANJOU

Loire

BURGUNDY

POITOU

AQUITAINE

GUIENNE

• Bordeaux

GASCONY

TOULOUSE

Pyrenees

THE ANGEVIN EMPIRE

POSSESSIONS OF HENRY II

NOMINAL POSSESSIONS OF KING OF FRANCE

LANDS RULED BY KING OF FRANCE

In 1173, the year Jocelin entered the abbey, Henry II's soldiers defeated the army of some rebel barons in a battle at Fornham, outside Bury's north gate. A fine sword of one of the rebel leaders has been found there in a ditch. Jocelin mentions this fighting in the very first sentence of a book he wrote twenty-five years later, when he had become one of the leading officials of the abbey.

He wrote this book because he was annoyed about the way Abbot Samson kept taking away the rights and powers of those officials, like himself, whose job it was to look after the monastery's property. Jocelin was in great difficulty, as monks are bound by three solemn vows. One of these is to be obedient to the head of the monastery, in this case Abbot Samson. Jocelin thought that by describing everything Samson had done over the past twenty-five years, he would at least be able to tell future generations of monks in his monastery what properly belonged to them as a group.

Jocelin was determined to show the monks how Samson had increased the abbot's own power and wealth at the monks' expense. He therefore wrote what is called *The Chronicle of Jocelin of Brakelond.* By the time he came to write it, he had learnt a simple, conversational, 'schoolboy' kind of Latin. It translates straight into spoken English in a way that the original Latin written by ancient Roman writers does not. He began at the beginning of his own life in the abbey. His own manuscript has not survived, but here you see the first page of a copy that was written in the abbey only a hundred years later. The page is numbered 121 because Jocelin's *Chronicle* was copied into a larger book that already had other things in it. The fact that it was copied and kept in the monks' library at Bury showed that Jocelin's plan was working. The generations of monks that followed him could always refer to his 'history' of the abbey in his day, and see whether things had changed very much in their time.

You can see the title (faint in the photograph because it was written in red ink): *Cronica Jocelini de Brakelond.* By saying the words aloud, and thinking of similar ones in English, you can make out the meaning of the first few words: *Quod vidi et audivi scribere curavi. . . .* 'What I saw and heard I took care to write, the bad things for a caution, the good ones for use, that happened in the church of St Edmund in our days, from the year when the men from Flanders were captured outside our town, and when I put on the religious habit. . .'.

Cronica Jocelin de Bakeloude

+ SES BENEDICIAS

By 'habit' Jocelin means the monks' distinctive dress which we will look at later. The 'men from Flanders' were mostly poor cloth-workers hired as troops by the rebel barons, and no use at fighting. They came for the loot because at home, in Flanders, they had heard that Bury was 'the best-provisioned place on earth'.

No picture survives of Jocelin, but the monk shown here with the money-bag and large keys must look very like Jocelin after he had become cellarer. (Jocelin would certainly have worn a beard most of the time, as the monks' rule was to shave five times a year.) The cellarer was responsible for keeping the monastery's cellars full of provisions. Cellars are store-houses, whether below or above ground, and at Bury included granaries, wool-stores and timber-yards. In the case of rich monasteries like St Edmund's, owning many lands and manors, the cellarer had charge of them, too.

This picture shows Adam, the cellarer of another great abbey—St Alban's in Hertfordshire. The painting appears in one of that monastery's books commemorating everyone who had been especially generous or useful to the abbey. Adam had earned himself a special burial-place among the abbots—under the floor of the chapter-house. This was because he had been particularly clever in increasing the rents of St Alban's abbey. Jocelin, as cellarer at Bury, not only looked after all the rents (a penny for each house in Bury, a penny for each cow pastured, and so on), and kept the keys to St Edmund's cellars, but he also wrote about it all, with all his heart, and so he is remembered also.

2. St. Edmund and the building of his abbey at Bury

To think about

1. How many people, from which countries outside England, had something to do with the abbey at Bury? What does this tell you about the separateness of England from Europe?

To find out

2. Apart from the idea of having a sort of 'holiday', find out some other reasons why people decided to go off on a pilgrimage.

3. Working either on your own or in a small group, make up a picture-story about St Edmund. Start with his murder by the Danes, and finish with pilgrims coming to pray at his shrine in Bury abbey. Put a sentence or two under each picture, and so make a story.

To do

4. Draw up an advertisement like those you see in papers and magazines, for a medieval pilgrimage, either to Compostela or to somewhere else.

5. Describe, as though you were a reporter, the procession moving Edmund's body from the round church to its new shrine in the abbey church. You can either write this as it would appear in a newspaper or record it on tape for radio or TV. If you record it, remember to include suitable 'background noises', such as bells ringing and monks singing.

6. Use the plans on pages 12 and 32 to help you to draw a simple plan showing the abbey church and the places mentioned on pages 12 and 13. Then draw a small picture to illustrate what used to happen in each of the places—the monks eating in the refectory, and so on. The pictures in this book will help you. Put the drawings in their proper place on the plan.

When Jocelin entered St Edmund's abbey, it was already 150 years old. In this chapter we look back to see how the abbey came into existence and grew so well. Even before the abbey came to be built, a small riverside town called *Bedericsworth* stood on that ground.

The town had an extremely ancient church of St Mary that later had to be moved to make way for one of the huge cross-wings of the Norman abbey-church where St Edmund's body lay (see plan on page 12). That older town and church belonged to the Anglo-Saxon kings of this part of England, then a separate kingdom called East Anglia.

The East Anglian ruling family, one of whom was commemorated by the burial of the famous treasure-ship at Sutton Hoo, soon accepted Christian beliefs. In their kingdom, a great many churches and monasteries were founded, including a small monastery, or minster, at Bedericsworth. Then the Danes invaded England in their long ships. A whole army came, complete with their horses, to see what they could plunder. The horses enabled them to move quickly among the farm-settlements and churches, to attack and rob at will. In the autumn of 869, the raiding army set up winter quarters at Thetford and defeated the East Anglian forces. On 20 November, they killed the East Anglian king, whose name was Edmund.

This happened at a place called *Haegelisdun*, or Hellesdon. It is probably the Hellesdon which is now a suburb of Norwich. The news spread that Edmund's body was riddled with arrows, and that the Danes had cut off his head and thrown it into the depths of Hellesdon Wood. When the Danes had gone, Edmund's people went to look for his head. They were guided to it by shouts of 'Here, here, here'—according to the story that quickly spread—and they found it being 'guarded' between the paws of a wolf. The story stated that the shouts came from Edmund's own lips. Probably, Edmund's grief-stricken followers heard these shouts of 'Here' coming from the people first on the scene, and they imagined the rest. We also guess that the wolf's plan may have been to eat the head, rather than to guard it! But we can understand King Edmund's unhappy people wanting to believe that Edmund, although defeated, could nevertheless work these 'miracles'.

They believed it so hard that it came to be accepted as the truth, as you can see from this drawing of the episode (and also from another on page 22). Naturally, when the head was found, it was rejoined to Edmund's body, as you see. It must have been 'embalmed', that is to say preserved, like an Egyptian mummy, with ointments made from the bark of certain trees. This drawing, made in 1433, shows Edmund's body, apparently still preserved and lying in its rich, jewelled shrine, or tomb, at Bury. He was now a saint.

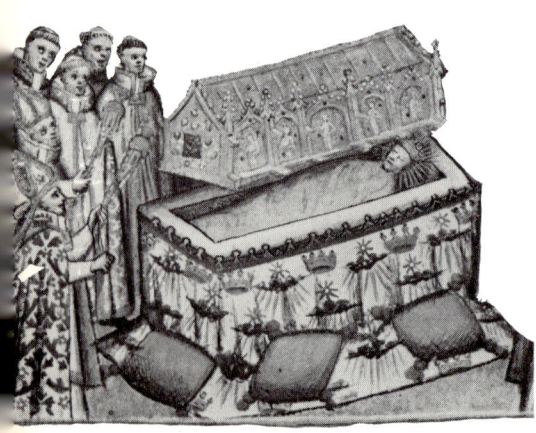

Not long after the Danes killed Edmund, they were forced by King Alfred and the west-countrymen to make peace and to accept Christianity. After that, Edmund seemed to all the English to have been a sort of hero of the 'Resistance' against the Danes. His body was fetched from the place where he was killed to the old royal East Anglian town of Bedericsworth. Many churches, all over England, were 'dedicated' to him. At Bedericsworth, the church where he lay began to be granted the rents and income from many estates. It acquired great rights and privileges, including the freedom to control its whole neighbourhood.

When new invasions were made by violent plunderers from the north, called Vikings, one of the Viking kings, Sweyn Forkbeard, decided to put an end to St Edmund's privileges. Luckily for the saint and for the chaplains who looked after his shrine, at that very moment Sweyn Forkbeard dropped dead! Edmund seemed better at defending himself after his death than when he was alive. After Sweyn's spectacular death, not even the strongest kings dared interfere with the saint's property and rights. Sweyn's son, King Cnut, decided to put monks in place of the chaplains who looked after the shrine. Monks, as we shall see, were more strictly religious men, living a daily religious routine. They built an abbey there, with the saint's tomb at the heart of their church. In this way, St Edmund's abbey began.

The abbey's first church, founded by King Cnut to hold Edmund's body, was a round wooden one. It is number 7 on the plan on page 12. In the time of Cnut, the town's name changed from Bedericsworth to Bury St Edmunds. Bury, or *burh* as it used to be spelt, means a fortified town, with gates and ramparts or walls. The drawing and photograph show how the wall defending the abbey itself was carried across the river beside the town's East Gate. You can see this also on the plan on page 32.

In William the Conqueror's time, the lord, or abbot, of St Edmund's abbey was called Baldwin. He arrived in Bury in 1065; before that he had been a monk at an abbey just outside Paris. Do you remember the square grid of the street-plan he gave Bury? He was perhaps remembering Paris, which also had a grid-pattern of streets, created there by the Romans.

From 1081 until he died in 1098, Abbot Baldwin organized the first part of the great rebuilding of St Edmund's abbey-church. In these years, his officers and masons completed the large, U-shaped end of the building. This was the whole *east end* of the church, which was always the most sacred part, with the high altar and the tombs and the relics of saints. When this part was finished, Edmund's body was brought from the round church and set in the place of honour at the heart of his new building.

Edmund was brought to his new shrine in 1095. After a halt of about seven years, the building work went on again with great energy until, in about 1140, all the parts shown on this plan were complete. The monk in charge of all the building work was called the *sacrist.* For the first twenty of those years the sacrist was Godfrey, a giant of a man 'but larger still in mind'. For the remaining years Ralph and Hervey, 'men of perfect judgement', were the sacrists.

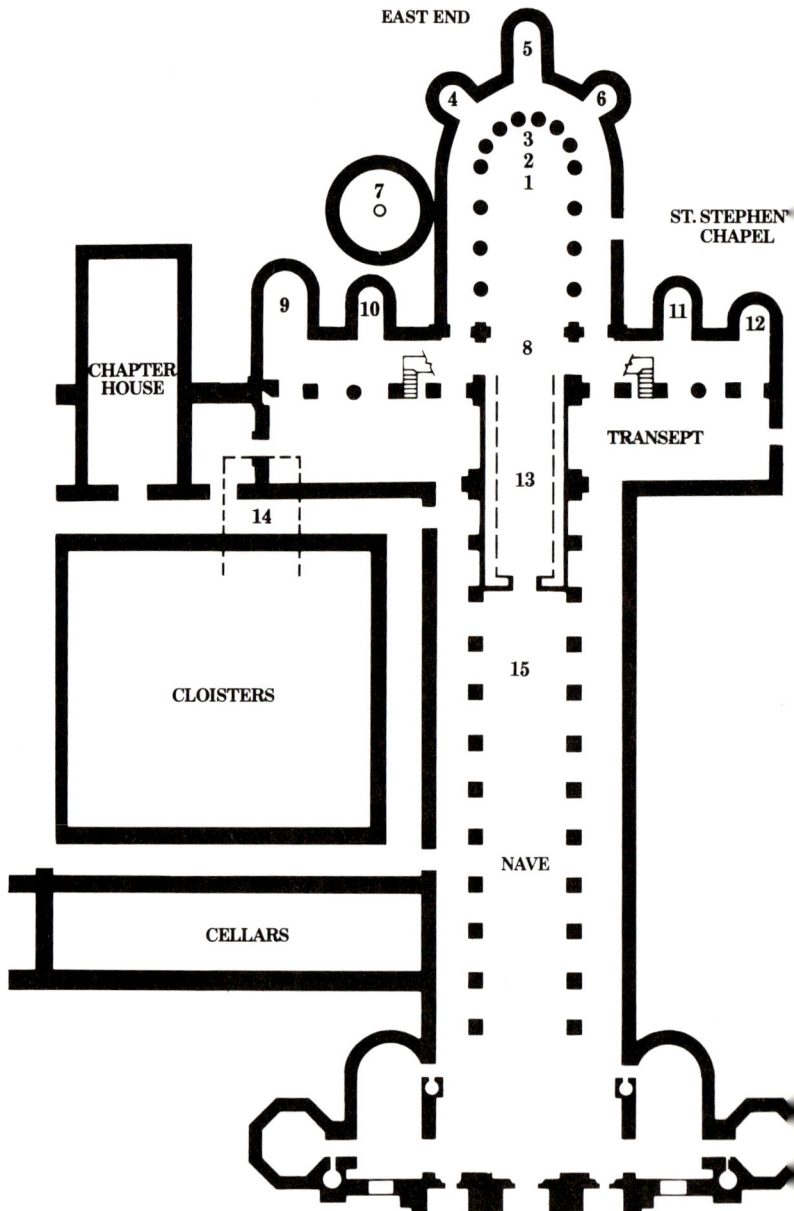

PLAN OF ABBEY CHURCH IN JOCELIN'S DAY

1	HIGH ALTAR	8	CHOIR-ALTAR
2	SHRINE OF ST. EDMUND	9	ST. MARTIN'S CHAPEL
3	ALTAR OF ST. THOMAS AND SHRINES OF ST. BOTULPH AND ST. JURMIN	10	ST. MARY'S CHAPEL
		11	ST. JOHN'S CHAPEL
		12	ST. NICHOLAS' CHAPEL
4	ST. SABA'S CHAPEL	13	MONKS' CHOIR
5	ST. NICASIUS' CHAPEL	14	SITE OF 7th–CENTURY
6	ST. PETER'S CHAPEL		MINSTER OF ST. MARY
7	'ROTUNDE' CHAPEL OF ST. EDMUND	15	ALTAR OF HOLY CROSS

Godfrey saw to the building of the *cloister* (a sort of square, draughty corridor, open in the middle, where the ordinary monks could read and occasionally talk), the *chapter-house* (for daily meetings), the *refectory* (for meals), the *dormitory* (for sleep), the *infirmary* (for the sick), and a new room for the abbot. Godfrey also built the cross-wings, or *transepts*, specially designed at Bury for the easy movement of crowds of visitors, the pilgrims to the shrines. A central tower went up where the transepts crossed, and a great bell was bought and hung in it. The nave, the long western body of the church, was also begun.

Ralph, and then Hervey, completed the nave, right up to the west front, more than 152 metres from the east front, a colossal size. They also built the tall stone walls round the edge of the whole monastery. St Mary's old church had stood in the way of the north wing of the new transept, so it was rebuilt where St Mary's parish church stands today. A new church of St James (now used as a cathedral) was built against the outer wall of the monastery. You can find both these churches on the plan on page 32.

By this time the abbot was Anselm, an Italian who had already been abbot of a monastery in Rome. He built this impressive gate-tower at the main approach to the new abbey-church. It plays an important part in Jocelin of Brakelond's story. The tower served as the main triumphal gateway to St Edmund's church and shrine; it also served as bell-tower to St James's parish church which stood alongside. Italians like to build towers for their church-bells. Can you see how Anselm's tower is like the one below, from Rome?

St James, one of Christ's chief friends and disciples, was believed to have visited Spain. At Compostela, in Spain, there was a shrine which was thought to contain his body: the shrine was one of the greatest centres of medieval pilgrimages which were, among other things, an early form of 'holidays abroad'. Abbot Anselm of Bury wanted to go to Compostela as a pilgrim, but was ordered to stay at Bury and look after St Edmund's abbey. So, instead, he built this tower in honour of St James.

Under Abbot Anselm, and in later years, one superb craftsman worked at Bury. He was not a monk, and we do not know where he came from. His name was Master Hugo. When the builders finally reached the west front of the church after almost forty years of building, Master Hugo made great double doors of bronze. These were designed for the middle one of three tall doorways. We can see only the outlines now in the rough flint-rubble front. 'As in other works Hugo surpassed everyone else, in the making of these doors he surpassed himself': so said the monks of his day.

3. In the abbey-church

To think about  1. What did the monks mean when they said that Master Hugo's ivory cross was 'incomparable'? (The middle of that word provides the clue.)

To find out  2. Find as many as you can of the ways in which the craftsmen of the Middle Ages adorned and decorated their churches. Books from your library will probably help. You may live near a very old church, where you can see for yourself.

To do  3. Make up, and act or tape-record, the conversation when Master Hugo discussed carving the ivory cross for the monks' choir with Helyas, the sacrist who got him to do the work. Hugo explains to the sacrist how he means to design the cross. The sacrist asks questions and makes suggestions.

 4. Pretend you are Master Hugo returning to the abbey-church today. Write down your feelings as you discover how much has vanished.

5. Use the pictures and information in this chapter to help you make a drawing of the west front of the abbey-church as it looked when it was new. It should include (a) the three tall doorways (b) Hugo's double bronze doors (c) carvings over the doors. You will be able to add to this drawing when you reach Chapter 6.

6. Model the Norman gate-tower out of boxes, using the pictures on pages 13, 14 and 15 to help you. Put in the arches and decoration. The upper openings are to let out the sound of the bells over the whole town.

We will try to imagine the abbey-church in which Jocelin spent so much of his life. We approach Anselm's new gate-tower, the one that he built instead of going to Compostela. First, do you see how its details remind you of this drawing of the gate of heaven?

Into it a winged angel is leading the people who have been good. They carry palm leaves, and one man wears a kind of crown. He may represent St Edmund himself. The drawing was probably made at Bury at about the same time as the building of Anselm's gate-tower.

Now cars are parked by the gate-tower, but can you make out the right-hand arch of the church-front beyond? Where Hugo's doors were, the arch is now filled with the small windows of a house. When Master Hugo's bronze doors were first hung, in about 1140, they were in the gleaming, creamy-yellow stone walls of the new main front of the church. The poor grey flinty walls in this photograph and the sad stumps that remain today of the rest of the abbey-church are only the rubble-core fillings of those beautiful new walls. All the smooth facing-stone was wrenched down and taken away when the monasteries were shut down by King Henry VIII.

Above: *The ruins of the abbey at Bury*
Below left: *Abbot Anselm's new gate tower*
Below right: *Houses built into the abbey ruins. Can you see the outline of the arch which once framed Hugo's bronze doors?*

We can only guess how Hugo's bronze doors looked. Several of the surviving bronze church-doors in Europe are from Jocelin's own day, thirty years after Hugo. Some famous earlier doors that Hugo might have known, and perhaps copied a little, are at Verona, in Italy. In these door-panels man's wickedness is shown: how Christ was betrayed and arrested by men with swords and staves; and how, in the beginning, Eve sat at her spinning, and Adam ploughed his fields, while one of their sons killed his brother.

When the bronze doors opened, you would see great avenues of stone, like these in Ely Cathedral today. The walls and pillars and window-glass were all richly coloured, like the Ely ceiling. At the far end, you knew you would find the shimmering, jewelled tomb of St Edmund and the shrines of other holy men. Almost at the far end of the *nave* (the first long section of the church) was a stone screen, dividing it from the *monks' choir* beyond (the plan is on page 12). The choir was where the eighty monks of St Edmund met to pray and to sing to God at regular intervals through the day, starting long before daybreak. At the far (east) end of their choir they had an altar. Then 21 metres beyond and above that stood the high altar of the abbey, with St Edmund's tomb immediately behind it.

Above and behind the high altar, and before St Edmund's shrine, was a great carved beam. Hanging from it, or perhaps standing on it, was a carved cross showing Christ's crucifixion. Smaller figures of his mother and St John stood at the foot of the cross. In the Middle Ages, the cross was called the *rood,* and the beam that carried it, the *rood-beam.* Jocelin notes that the smaller figures had been enriched with a great weight of gold and silver by an archbishop. They were brought with Edmund from the old round church.

The monks' choir had its own altar and its own crucifixion scene, carved by Master Hugo. Master Hugo's cross is thought to be the one which reappeared dramatically in 1963 from the cellars of a bank in Switzerland. It is now in a New York museum. Apart from Anselm's great gate-tower and several books that were already in use in the abbey, the only object that survives almost exactly as it was in Jocelin's day is this cross.

It is carved in yellow ivory from walrus-tusks. In about 1150, the Bury monks recorded that a cross for their choir was 'made incomparably by the hand of Master Hugo'. How we came to think that it may be this one, found in Switzerland, is a long and complicated detective story.

The hanging figure of Christ that was pegged on to the front of the cross has now been found at Oslo in Norway.

On the left arm of the cross, Hugo's carving shows the strange scene at Christ's tomb, as it is described in the Gospels. The same subject was drawn by someone else at Bury, a much less clever artist than Hugo, but at about the same time as he was carving his cross. What differences do you notice? The women have brought jars of scent. The soldiers guarding the tomb have collapsed at the sight of the angel. In the carving, the whole design is simpler. Only five soldiers are shown. Can you find them all? The sword at the foot of the drawing is just like the one in the ivory. In the ivory, the angel has been joined by the figure of the risen Christ.

In the centre of the cross, a scene shows Moses, the earliest leader of the Jews, leading them out of captivity in Egypt. This is the theme of some of Hugo's best paintings in one of the books that Jocelin must often have looked at—the Bury Bible. We look at that in the next chapter.

4. Among the abbey's books

To think about  1. Writing was done in the scriptorium. *How many words are there which have something to do with writing, and which have* scrip *or* scrib *somewhere in them?*

To find out  2. *Write about all the different ways you can find in which the stories of Christianity could be given to people. A few would be able to read, but most would not.*

 3. *Design you own initial as though it was a letter in one of the books made by the monks. You can get some ideas from the capital C in the picture on page 27.*

To do  4. *Make up four entries in an imaginary diary kept by Boston of Bury when he was travelling about, listing books in monasteries. Say something about the libraries of other monasteries, and how they compared with his own library at Bury. You can find more about his life in the* Dictionary of National Biography.

 5. *Make up a modern rhyme, of eight or nine lines, like the one in this chapter, about the way you think you should behave today. On no account write it in the cover of a library-book as the Bury monk did!*

 6. *Make a quill pen, like those the monks used, from a good tough feather, and try writing with it.*

The monks' library was an important part of the abbey at Bury. Although the buildings of the abbey were largely destroyed under Henry VIII, the books were distributed among local families and university men. Many of these books still survive today in Cambridge and other libraries. At the top of page 21 is a picture of the library at Hereford Cathedral.

Master Hugo's great Bible still carries the number B.1. that it was given when it was in the monks' library at Bury. We do not know where their first library-room was, nor when it was built. (In a later century it was built above the novices' schoolroom, near the north-east corner of the chapter-house.)

Not only have many books survived, but so have some of the old catalogues. The earliest list of Bury's books was made before the Normans came in 1066. It tells us that nine service-books were in the church and also a copy of the *Life of St Edmund.* Some of those first monks at Bury had a book or two of their own, and out at one of the abbey's manor-houses there were thirty books, not counting those used for the services.

The next catalogue dates from Jocelin's day and shows that by then there were at least 136 volumes in the abbey. They included Hugo's great Bible. It was used in the refectory. One of the monks read aloud from it, while the others ate in silence. Two centuries later, about 1410, Bury abbey had a librarian called John Boston, sometimes known as 'Boston de Bury' or 'Boston of Bury'. He became famous because he travelled round all the monasteries of England, listing their books.

This picture shows Hugo's painting of Moses in the great Bible that was already being used thirty years before Jocelin entered the abbey. The Bible tells us that the Jews escaped from Egypt around the Sinai peninsula. Moses came down from Mount Sinai and told them about the Ten Commandments that God had given him while he was in the clouds at the mountain-top. God had written these Commandments on two tablets of stone—which Moses holds to his right side.

The story of Moses was first written in Hebrew, the Jews' language. It described how Moses' face glowed when he came from the mountain. As the Hebrew word for 'glowed' is the same as for 'horns', artists in the Middle Ages often showed Moses with these curious horns. (A monk has also scribbled the name *Moises.*)

Here Moses has gathered the 'children of Israel' together to tell them God's word about which animals they may eat for food and which they must not. Hugo shows a boy listening wide-eyed to what Moses says. The animals on the far left seem to be listening too.

At Bury, each book had a 'press-mark', as it does in a modern library. That is, it was grouped or 'classed' with other books on the same subject, and given a letter and a number. For example, books by or about St Augustine were given the letter A. Bury had fifty-two of these. Class B began with the books of the Bible.

C included all the chronicles. Jocelin's was copied into the book that is still numbered C.28. M included the medical books and S the sermons. All the psalters would have been with the other service-books in the church, not in the library. Psalters contained the Psalms of King David and were set to the music of the harp. *Psalterium* is the old word for a harp.

All these books were made before printing was invented. They were written by hand, usually in a room called the *scriptorium*. In the picture on the right you can see the scribe Eadwine, who lived at Canterbury, taking great care over writing his book. In Jocelin's time, two water-mills beside the river, below Bury, were rented from the abbey by a man called Gervase. The rent that he paid to the monks was regularly spent on buying parchment and ink for their scriptorium. The parchment on which they wrote was made from the specially treated skins of sheep or goats.

When Master Hugo made his great Bible, he could not obtain parchment good enough for his paintings and so he sent to the Scots for the best vellum. Vellum is fine parchment, prepared from the skins of calves, lambs or kids (young goats). The Scots then were the people of Scotland *and* Ireland. Very fine illustrated writing had been done in Ireland for a long time.

Can you see where a torn piece in the edge of the vellum in a page of Hugo's Bible was neatly repaired two or three hundred years after Hugo's time? Another monk, with a sense of humour, has drawn a king's head on the white vellum where the repair was made. It is St Edmund's head, saying *hic hic hic* which is the Latin for *here here here.* Do you remember the legend of St Edmund's head (see page 10)? This is a nice sign that Edmund's monks thought about that story as they sat reading the splendid books in their library at Bury.

This picture from a twelfth century manuscript shows the sort of watermill that Gervase would have rented from Bury Abbey.

Christ driving from the temple the money-changers and men selling oxen, sheep and doves for sacrifice. Can you see the animals and doves, and the coins falling off the table? 'Make not my Father's house a house of merchandise.'

The Bury monks have left other signs of the way they used their books. The drawing of the scene outside Christ's tomb, which we compared with Hugo's ivory carving, was just one of a whole set of drawings. Two more are shown here. They were all bound into a volume of the New Testament given to the abbey by Reginald of Denham (Denham is a village near Bury). Someone who was reading the book in the library in the fourteenth century practised his geography by writing down, on the inside of the front cover, the names of places scattered all over the known world. Then, underneath that, someone else reading this New Testament a whole century later scribbled some rhymes, probably from memory. These rhymes had been made by a Bury monk, John Lydgate, to help boys and monks to remember how to behave politely. Translated into a more modern English they read like this:

Be straight, dear boy, look not aside,
Turning not round to gaze at all.
Don't stand with your back propping up the wall.
Pick not your nose and, above all,
Be alert.
Before your master, do not scratch nor squirm,
And if he speaks to you, in any place,
Look at him cheerfully in the face, not glumly down.
Try to walk calmly when you're in the town.

In Solomon's porch in the Temple in Jerusalem, the Jews prepare to stone Jesus. They feel angry because they do not understand him when he says: 'Any one of us can be a god as soon as we understand the word of God.'

The dancing lady on the left is not at all calm. These three pictures are taken from one of the oldest books in the abbey library. They were drawn in the tenth century, not long after the Danes killed St Edmund. They too are about behaviour, and they show the result of bad behaviour. First, the lady dances wildly. Then she prances on horseback with too much pride and so she is thrown from her horse. You can just see the Latin word for pride, *superbia* (shortened in medieval handwriting to *supbia*) on the left. The original Roman book from which this was copied may have been brought to England from Rome by one of the early missionaries—possibly by St Felix, the first missionary to East Anglia.

In Jocelin's day pictures like these above, from a church wall at Chaldon in Surrey, were painted on church walls so that people who could not read could learn from them instead. This picture warns us that we will be punished for bad behaviour in hell. The people in the middle are trying to climb the ladder to heaven, but those who do not keep their eyes on God are pulled into hell by the demons. There they are burned in a boiling pot or made to work on a sharp saw. In the top left-hand picture, St Michael is weighing people's good behaviour against their bad, to see if they deserve to go to heaven. What is happening in the fourth picture?

25

5. Daily life

To think about

 1. Why would it be sensible for a boy to spend a little time in a monastery before he became a monk?

 2. Why were the monks of Bury abbey jealous of the Grey Friars, refusing to let them stay in the town?

To find out

 3. Use the information in this chapter to work out an illustrated timetable of an average day in the life of a monk at Bury abbey.

 4. From local guide-books and reference-books, try to collect a list of all the monasteries in any part of the British Isles you know. Write them out in groups according to the Rule they followed, e.g. Benedictines, Augustinians. You could also mark them on a map.

To do

 5. Make up, and act with some friends, the daily meeting of the monks in the chapter-house. Include a boy asking to be admitted as a novice, and two monks confessing their faults.

 6. Perhaps you or your teacher could find a record of some of the chants the monks used in their services. Listen to them and imagine yourself a monk. Which parts of your life would you like and which would you dislike?

When Jocelin was going to join the abbey, he first of all spent three days learning about it. As there were no hotels, travellers used to be allowed to stay at monasteries. Look at the people on the right enjoying a meal. At Bury, anybody who was not a monk or priest was supposed to stay in the abbot's guest-house but, since the old abbot at that time was failing to carry out this duty, Jocelin slept for those three nights in the monks' guest-house.

On each of the three days, he had to appear in front of all the monks at their business-meeting in the chapter-house and ask to be admitted as a novice. After being accepted on the third day, he was dressed in his monk's 'habit' and began his year's training.

Over his underclothes he wore a long *tunic* down to his feet, a *girdle* (belt), a *scapula* (a sort of apron covering the tunic back and front), a *hood* (usually attached to the scapula), and a *cowl* (an overall, with wide sleeves, also reaching to the feet). The habit of Benedictine monks, like those at Bury, was made of black wool, so they were often called Black Monks. They followed the Rule of St Benedict, that a monastery should be 'a school for the service of God'.

Jocelin's *novice-master* during his training was a monk called Samson: he later became abbot and played the chief part in the *Chronicle* that Jocelin wrote. Jocelin learned the Rule and learned the psalms by heart and how to sing them in 'plain-chant'. Then he took his *vows.* He promised to stay in Bury abbey for the rest of his life and to 'amend his manners' (try to live a life without fault). He promised not to acquire worldly wealth ('vow of poverty'), not to marry ('vow of chastity') and, above all, he vowed to be obedient. He had to spend several hours a day chanting and praying with the eighty other monks in their *choir.* In that way they hoped to please God and make Him kind to all the people in the world outside.

St Benedict's Rule was also followed by women. They were called nuns. By 1400, there were nearly 300 Benedictine monasteries and 100 nunneries in England alone. There were other *Orders* also. The men on the left singing from a book (they are painted inside a capital-letter C) were called Augustinian canons. They followed the Rule of St Augustine, which let them go outside the monastery more, to preach and run hospitals. Here you see them in Christchurch, Dublin. The capital C stands for *Canto.* This Latin word means 'I sing' or 'I chant'. You can see that 'chant' is almost the same as the Latin word. Can you read the notes of music over the C?

Soon after Jocelin's time, the followers of St Francis, known as Grey Friars, tried to settle in Bury but they were driven out by the jealous monks. In towns where they were not driven out, these friars worshipped God in their choir, but they also believed in going out and preaching among the people. Here you see ten of them during a service in the choir. You can tell from their faces that they would rather be out preaching. They know the service by heart.

You can tell that they are Grey Friars by their belts—the white cord of St Francis—and by their sandals. Monks like Jocelin wore boots, not sandals. For their services in the night they put on 'night-boots' which were cloth slippers. Under their habits they wore a shirt, underpants and socks. An official called the chamberlain saw that these were washed at the *laundry.* He also supplied lambskins and catskins when the monks had to sit in the open cloister in winter.

St Benedict's monks, like Jocelin, had taken the vow of poverty and could own no private possessions, but a Benedictine abbey (by which we mean the abbot and his monks as a group) sometimes acquired great wealth, as we have seen at Bury. By giving lands to an abbey, people hoped to please God and his saints. However, the lands had to be farmed, the rents collected and the work managed, and in this way St Benedict's Rule for his monks was weakened. He wanted them to concentrate on serving God in their thoughts and their singing in church. He wanted them to have enough to eat and drink to be able to do their work properly and stand the long hours in church. He did not want them to be bothered with the outside world. Yet the more popular the abbeys were, the more people heaped gifts upon them. By the time Jocelin came on the scene, Bury abbey had great estates but it was deep in debt, and worry.

In Italy, St Francis of Assisi was living at the same time as Jocelin. A rich young man, he gave away everything he had. Like many young people today, he saw his riches as an obstacle between him and all poor people, and between him and God. Without the worries of wealth and property, he felt that he was the brother of everyone and of every living thing. His most famous sermon he preached to the birds. His favourite saying was 'Foxes have holes, birds have nests, but the Son of Man [Jesus] has nowhere to lay his head.' In Assisi, several rich young people came under his influence. One was Clare (later St Clare) who founded a house of nuns, living wholly without possessions. You can see her on the left.

St Francis's Grey Friars and St Clare's Minoresses, or Poor Clares, spread quickly all over Europe. It is easy to see how the monks of Bury felt threatened by them: Bury abbey had great possessions, but these people were preaching that it was better to be poor—and so they were kept out of the town.

The Grey Friars and the Minoresses made their famous attempt to reform religious life with their belief in simplicity and poverty, but then they themselves, over the years, were spoiled by their own success.

Before the time of St Francis and St Clare, other famous reformers introduced new rules for monks and nuns and new forms of monastic life. There were Cluniacs, who began their reform at Cluny, in France. There were the Carthusians, who started at Chartreuse and whose monasteries in England are called the Charterhouses. We have already noticed the Augustinian canons and the Rule of St Augustine (page 27).

The best-remembered of the reformed monasteries in England are those of the Cistercians. The name comes from the place Cîteaux in Burgundy (France). These monks believed very strongly in the simple life. This led them to build their monasteries far away from town life. They preferred the wild, remote countryside, which they tamed and farmed. This is how the great abbeys of Fountains and Rievaulx came to be built so deep in the Yorkshire Dales, and why their ruins are so big and so interesting. You can see a plan of Rievaulx Abbey and its ruins here.

While Jocelin was one of about eighty monks at Bury, the Cistercian abbey at Rievaulx had 140 enthusiastic monks and 600 'lay-brothers'. The lay-brothers lived in the abbey but worked on the surrounding farms. The great Cistercian reformer was St Bernard, who insisted that the abbey buildings must be plain and without any unnecessary decoration. Nothing must distract the monks' minds from God.

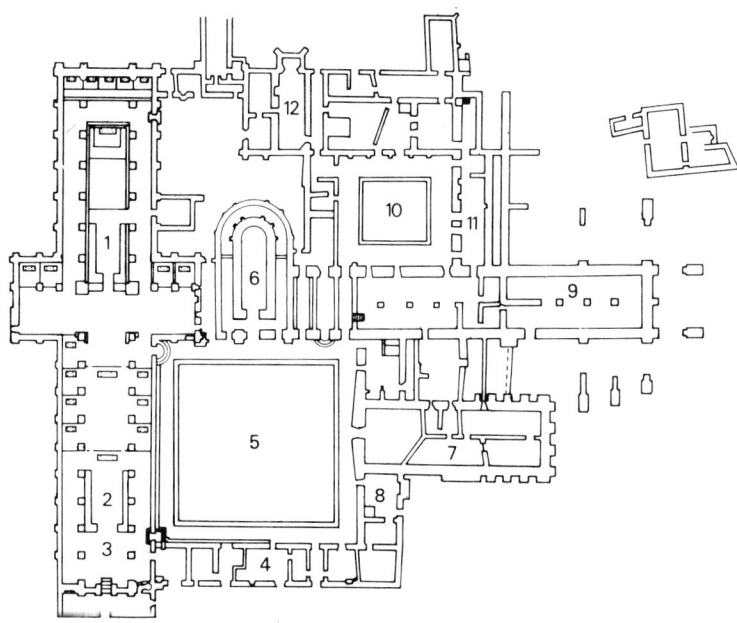

1 Choir
2 Lay-brothers' choir
3 Nave
4 Lay-brothers' rooms
5 Cloister
6 Chapter-house
7 Refectory
8 Kitchen
9 Novices' rooms
10 Infirmary cloister
11 Reredorter or communal lavatories, kept clean by a channel of running water
12 Abbot's lodging

You may feel that your timetable at school is full enough. Here is the timetable Jocelin had to keep when he was an ordinary monk. (He was excused from some of the services when he became an official later on, and had to manage the estates.) During the winter, his day started at about 2 o'clock in the morning and went on till about 7 o'clock in the evening, 8 o'clock in summer. Then he would go up to sleep in the *dormitory.* Here is a dormitory that survives from a Somerset abbey. Try to picture beds along both sides.

The monks slept in their habits. At 2 A.M. one of them woke the others. They put on their night-boots and went down into the choir. Prayers and psalms lasted until the dawn. Next came reading in the cloister till 8 A.M. Then the monks went back to the dormitory to change into day-boots, and down to the *lavatory* (wash-room) to wash their faces and comb their hair, before going back into the choir.

Next came the daily meeting in the *chapter-house,* where part of St Benedict's Rule was read. (On the left is the chapter-house of Bristol Cathedral.) At the meeting, confessions of faults were made. A wrongdoer had to sit all day in public in the nave of the church with his cowl over his face: when a procession passed by, he had to lie full-length on the floor. A less serious wrongdoer had to sit on a low stool in front of all the monks at their meeting in the chapter-house. After these confessions, the monks heard the news of the day and discussed any of the monastery's business that might affect them all. Jocelin says a lot in his *Chronicle* about what went on in these chapter-meetings.

After this, the day's work lasted from about 9.30 until 12.30. This was the period when books were studied and written, when works of art were made, and when the officials got on with their work of managing the monastery and all its estates. At about 12.30 all went back into the choir for the main service of the day, the High Mass. At last, at about 2 P.M., they went to the *refectory* for the first and main meal of the day—twelve hours after getting out of bed. Hands were washed before meals: there was a lavatory for this in the cloister near the refectory. The picture shows a fine one that survives at Gloucester cathedral.

The meal was plain and simple and the monks would certainly be ready for it. From 3 P.M. till 5 P.M. there was more reading, then evening service in the choir and, finally, night-boots on. Once a week there was feet-washing, when the feet of some poor people were washed too. A drink or a light supper came before bed. Then a few hours later the whole routine began all over again.

The monks had a hard day. What work is this monk doing? As Bury was a rich monastery, the monks were fairly well looked after. Do you remember (page 4) how Domesday Book described seventy-five townspeople working for the monks? By Jocelin's time there were well over a hundred. When he came to manage the *cellars,* he was in charge of forty-nine servants. They included his hall-steward, a hall-cleaner, the goldsmith, two gardeners, a mower, a pantry-boy, five cooks (two with the title 'Master'), and John Pug, who made the sauce.

The *sacrist* had twenty-four servants. The *chamberlain* omployed Geoffrey the shoemaker, Simon the 'pelterer' (who prepared skins and furs for wearing), Walter the tailor and his man, Robert the washerman, and Ralph and Job the bathmen. (We do not know how often the monks bathed: if they each had one bath every fortnight, that would mean preparing the bath four times a day.) Nine servants worked in the infirmary, ten helped the *almoner* to look after the poor, and seven looked after the guest-house under the *guest-master.*

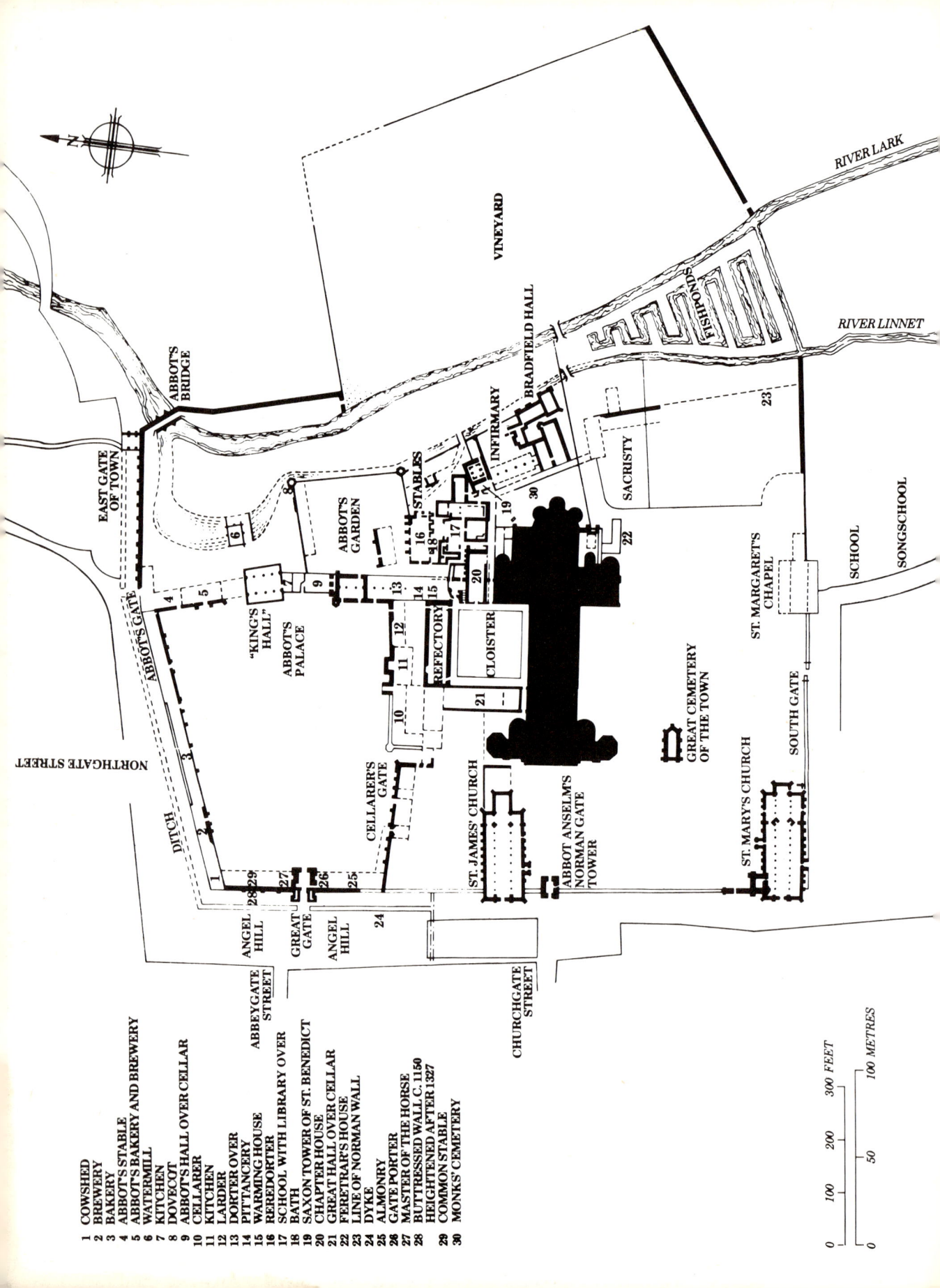

RIVER LARK

RIVER LINNET

VINEYARD

FISHPONDS

BRADFIELD HALL

INFIRMARY

SACRISTY

SCHOOL

SONGSCHOOL

ST. MARGARET'S CHAPEL

SOUTH GATE

ST. MARY'S CHURCH

GREAT CEMETERY OF THE TOWN

ABBOT ANSELM'S NORMAN GATE TOWER

ST. JAMES' CHURCH

CHURCHGATE STREET

ANGEL HILL

GREAT GATE

CELLARER'S GATE

REFECTORY

CLOISTER

ANGEL HILL

ABBEYGATE STREET

NORTHGATE STREET

DITCH

ABBOT'S GATE

"KING'S HALL"

ABBOT'S PALACE

ABBOT'S GARDEN

STABLES

EAST GATE OF TOWN

ABBOT'S BRIDGE

N

300 FEET

100 METRES

1 COWSHED
2 BREWERY
3 BAKERY
4 ABBOT'S STABLE
5 ABBOT'S BAKERY AND BREWERY
6 WATERMILL
7 KITCHEN
8 DOVECOT
9 ABBOT'S HALL OVER CELLAR
10 CELLARER
11 KITCHEN
12 LARDER
13 DORTER OVER
14 PITTANCERY
15 WARMING HOUSE
16 REREDORTER
17 SCHOOL WITH LIBRARY OVER
18 BATH
19 SAXON TOWER OF ST. BENEDICT
20 CHAPTER HOUSE
21 GREAT HALL OVER CELLAR
22 FERETRAR'S HOUSE
23 LINE OF NORMAN WALL
24 DYKE
25 ALMONRY
26 GATE PORTER
27 MASTER OF THE HORSE
28 BUTTRESSED WALL C. 1150
   HEIGHTENED AFTER 1327
29 COMMON STABLE
30 MONKS' CEMETERY

Above: *Plan of Bury St Edmunds abbey including buildings that were added after Jocelin's time.*
Below: *An aerial view of the abbey ruins and the town of Bury St Edmunds.*

Altogether, over a hundred servants worked in the abbey in Jocelin's day, as well as the abbot's own household. All these people lived in the town, not in the abbey itself. The town was controlled by the sacrist. Its first function was to serve and supply the abbey, but it was growing fast, like other towns. It had a prosperous market and a famous fair. When Jocelin was at Bury, this fair was held in the summer, as part of the festival of St James. People came to it from London and from all over Europe too. The big church in the photograph on page 33 is St James's, with Abbot Anselm's Norman tower beside it. The open space, with all the parked cars, is Angel Hill, where the fair used to be held. All the profits from the fair, like those from the markets, went to the abbey.

The street running from the Norman tower to the left across the foot of the photograph is called Churchgate Street. (Find it on the map on page 2). If you walk up this street, leaving the tower behind you, you come to a right-angled crossing (near the left edge of the photograph). Turn right, into what is now called Hatter Street. When Jocelin was alive, this was called Heathenman's Street. It was the Jewish part of the town.

At the top of Heathenman's Street, turn right towards the cars on Angel Hill. When Jocelin knew this road, it was 'Cook Row', where the cooks lived. Go straight on to Angel Hill, cross over and go through the great square gate that led to the abbot's palace. Inside the gate, turn left and you are facing the place where the bakehouse stood. (Find this on the plan on page 32). As well as all the loaves baked for the monks and the guest-house and the infirmary, ninety-four loaves of three different qualities were baked each day for the abbey's servants. The best ones went to the tanner, the chief baker, the scribe and four of the chaplains (priests who were not monks). Second-class loaves went to the chief stableman, the swineherd, the miller, the woodwarden, the brewer, the fisherman, the cheeseman, the chaplain of the Round Chapel, the mustardman and the embroiderer. (Not long after Jocelin's time, Mabel of Bury St Edmunds was one of the most famous embroiderers in the world.) Third-class loaves went to people like the infirmary cook and the blood-letter, whose work Jocelin mentions. And now, after seeing how and where he lived, we can turn at last to his story.

A bag of corn is brought to the mill to be ground.

r gtre mont facoillent la uolec

6. Jocelin's story: the election of Abbot Samson

To think about

 1. What does this chapter tell you about Samson which makes you think he would be a good choice for abbot?

To find out

 2. Find Bishops Waltham on a road-map of England. Then, supposing that they went by the Icknield Way, decide how the monks from Bury would have got there. If you can get a copy of the Ordnance Survey Map of Roman Britain, use that to work out an alternative route by the surviving Roman roads. Work out roughly how far this journey was.

 3. Look up Thomas à Becket in other books and find out something about his murder in Canterbury cathedral. In particular, try to find out how King Henry II was in some way to blame for the crime.

To do

 4. Imagine you are one of the monks who went to Bishops Waltham for the new abbot's election. You are not supposed to talk about life in the world outside the monastery, but take a chance and write a letter to a friend back home at Bury, describing (a) the journey (b) the meeting with the king (c) the election itself.

Jocelin's story begins in 1173, with his own start at the abbey. Abbot Hugh was getting old. He was a good monk but a feeble abbot and no use at managing the abbey's estates and money-matters. St Benedict's Rule was strictly obeyed, and God was honoured in the regular services of the monks' choir, but this rich abbey was deep in debt.

Twenty years earlier, a fire had destroyed the refectory, dormitory, chapter-house and infirmary, and the abbot's hall, all of which had not long been built. They were all rebuilt at once, by a sacrist called Helyas. (It was for Helyas that Master Hugo carved the ivory cross.) When Abbot Hugh became abbot in 1157, he probably started in debt, with all the new building to be paid for. By the time Jocelin arrived, as a novice, the abbey's affairs were in a very poor way.

Borrowing money was the only solution that Abbot Hugh could think of. Every half-year, one or two hundred pounds were added to the debt.

'I saw a "promise-to-pay" given to Isaac, the son of Rabbi Joce, for £400, but I don't know what for. And I saw another given to Benedict the Jew of Norwich for £880... We had owed Benedict another debt for fourteen years. In all, we owed him £1200, not counting all the greatly increased interest. . . . Then the cellarer, without telling the rest of the monks, owed £60 to Jurnet, Benedict's brother.' (To get an idea of the value of the debts in modern money, multiply by a hundred.)

The Jews were protected by the king because he could claim the wealth of any Jew who died. Christians who owed money to a Jew could gain by his death, as the king rarely claimed from *them* their debt to that Jew. Fifty-seven Jews were massacred in Bury on Palm Sunday in 1190; this was perhaps connected with the fact that a lot of Christians owed the Jews money.

The drawing above shows the unpopularity of the rich Jews named by Jocelin. It was drawn by one of the king's tax-collectors on a tax account-roll. It shows Isaac, the son of Jurnet of Norwich, at the top, with three faces and wearing the crown of the Demon King. A devil points out two of his money-lending friends.

During his first year Jocelin asked Master Samson, his novice-master, about all this borrowing and debt.

' ''Why don't you speak out against it? You fear God more than you fear men, and have nothing to lose. You are not hoping for promotion, to become one of the abbey's officials.'' (Jocelin was writing down this conversation long after Samson had become abbot, so it is a kind of joke.) Samson replied: ''My son, a child just burnt is afraid of fire. Abbot Hugh jailed me, and banished me to Castle Acre in Norfolk for criticising him and standing up for our common good. This is the dark hour, when only flatterers are heard.'' '

From the start, Jocelin was learning how difficult it was to keep that most important vow of obedience.

In September 1180, old Abbot Hugh decided that a few days' pilgrimage would do him no harm. He was wrong. He set out for Canterbury, to the tomb of St Thomas à Becket, King Henry II's archbishop of Canterbury who had been murdered in his cathedral ten years earlier. When Abbot Hugh was near Rochester, he fell and his knee-cap stuck in the muscles above the knee. The doctors made it worse and he died in November. No one seemed sorry.

Two monks were chosen to cross the sea to Normandy to tell King Henry II about the abbot's death. One of these was Master Samson. The abbey was governed by the *prior* until a new abbot could be appointed. Samson was still the *sub-sacrist,* which meant that he was in charge of the building-workmen. He made sure that all building repairs were done quickly. That pleased the other monks. He also built an outer wall round the monks' choir-enclosure and arranged for Bible-story scenes to be painted all round it. There were ninety of these pictures, all stories from the Book of Genesis. Samson also wrote sad verses to go with each painting and luckily these were copied down before the paintings were destroyed. Some of them match word-for-word the messages that Master Hugo carved on the ivory cross in the choir: Samson must have known the cross well.

Feeling against the Norwich Jews was already strong in 1144 when a boy, William, died and was believed to have been crucified by them, as in this picture. He soon became 'Saint' William.

He also had tons of stone and sand brought to Bury for the building of the great tower over the west end of the church.

It must have looked very like the great tower at the west end of Ely Cathedral (not counting the top storey of Ely's tower). Samson got the first stage of Bury's tower built while he was sub-sacrist. From a hollow tree-trunk he made a money-box to collect money for the building of the tower from visitors who came to the abbey and St Edmund's shrine. In that way he avoided borrowing any more money from the Jews, who naturally did not like this sub-sacrist, Samson.

The Jews had some control over Samson's superior, the sacrist, who even allowed them to keep their huge piles of money in the safety of the abbey's *treasury.* He also allowed their wives and children to take shelter in the *pittancery,* a safe hide-out in the middle of the abbey, when there was bad feeling between the Jews and the Christian townspeople. Jocelin saw what difficulties this caused from the point of view of Christian monks and he notes how weak the prior was during this time.

The Jews persuaded the king's steward at Bury to stop Samson using the money collected from the people for building. It had to go towards paying off the debt to the Jews.

Jocelin describes how the monks now began to pray to God for a suitable new abbot. Three times a week they lay at full length on the floor of the choir in an effort to please God; and they began to discuss the kind of abbot they wanted. Jocelin shows how little our characters have changed over the centuries. He once saw Samson sitting and listening to a group of monks during their blood-letting that took place every Spring and Autumn. It was thought good for their health to lose some blood, so they went to the infirmary to be bled, and their routine was made easier for about three days.

'At such times, the monks would reveal the secret of their hearts,' said Jocelin. 'I saw Samson sitting, and smiling, without a word, and noting the words of each monk. And I heard him repeat some of their opinions twenty years later, when he was abbot.'

At last, in February 1182, King Henry II sent to Bury for the prior and twelve monks to appear before him at Bishops Waltham, near Winchester, to elect a new abbot. Excited, all the monks assembled in the chapter-house at Bury. The prior chose twelve to go with him, and everyone approved. Six others were then picked, as good judges, to select three candidates for abbot and write down their names. These names were put into a sealed box to be taken to Bishops Waltham for the king to choose one of them. The group set out on foot, probably along the old prehistoric road south, the Icknield Way.

'Samson brought up the rear. As sub-sacrist he carried the money for their expenses, and also the official letters for the king, hung in a case round his neck, as though he was their only servant. Catching up his long habit over his arms, he followed the rest at a distance.'

The remains of King Henry's castle at Bishops Waltham. The modern wooden steps on the right lead up to the great hall in which Samson was chosen to be abbot.

Seal showing Henry II alert and ready to do justice.

When King Henry swore 'by God's eyes' this picture from Toulouse of a majestic 'all-seeing' Christ is the sort of image he had in mind.

After many delays and difficulties (for it was February), they arrived at King Henry's castle. Henry II was a well-built man with terrific energy, his red-gold hair now becoming grey and thin. He must have liked St Edmund's abbey, as it was there that his chief rival, Eustace of Blois, died suddenly in 1153. Henry and Eustace had fought bitterly for the throne and at last, in 1154, Henry could become king without any more trouble. (Eustace had been robbing St Edmund's abbey. This was a dangerous thing to do, as King Cnut's father had found out.)

So the great King Henry received the thirteen kindly and asked for the names of three from their monastery. They opened the case they had brought, broke the seal and found the three names, with Samson's at the top. The prior and others of higher rank than Samson blushed because their names were not among the three. The king said that he did not know these three and he asked for three more names from Bury, and three from other monasteries, to make nine in all. Slowly, seven names were struck out and two were left—the prior and Samson.

'The Bishop of Winchester, who was present, asked them about these two men, and said, "Tell me openly, do you wish to have Samson?" The majority answered clearly, "We want Samson." Then the king spoke: "I will do what you want. But watch out. For, by the eyes of God, if you're making a mistake I shall be upon you."

Samson, elected, fell at the king's feet and kissed them. He swiftly rose, and swiftly moved to the altar with the others from Bury, singing Psalm 51, "Have mercy upon me, O God, according to thy loving kindness". His head was held high, and the expression on his face never changed. When the king saw this, he said to those standing nearby, "By God's eyes this man we've elected thinks himself worthy to be in charge of his abbey." '

7. Jocelin's story: the good years under Abbot Samson

 **To think about**

1. What were all the things that Samson did to make the abbey at Bury stronger and richer again?

2. What would Samson be trying to show everybody by ordering a new seal, and not using Abbot Hugh's old one?

 **To find out**

3. Pretend to be a newspaper or TV reporter describing the scene at Bury when Samson returned there on Palm Sunday. You can write your description, or record it, using suitable noises in the background.

 **To do**

4. Use the pictures in this book to help you draw Abbot Samson's strange dream, which Jocelin describes on this page.

5. Model Moyses Hall, using the picture on page 43 to help you.

The abbot of Peterborough at the time of Samson

What sort of a man was the new abbot of Bury? Here is Jocelin's account of the strange dream which set Samson on the road to becoming a monk. People in those days took their dreams very seriously and tried to explain them. Indeed, many people still try to do this.

'He told me once, that when he was a boy of nine, in Norfolk, he dreamt that he was standing before the great tower-gateway of St Edmund's church at Bury, and that the Devil reached out his arms and tried to catch him. He shouted out in his sleep, ''St Edmund help me'', though he had never heard his name before. His mother was amazed to hear him. She took him to St Edmund's abbey so that he could pray there. And when they came to the tower-gate he said, ''Mother! that's the place, that's the gate I saw in my dream, where the Devil tried to catch me.'' He said he recognised the place as clearly as if he had seen it with his own eyes. The abbot himself explained his dream like this: the Devil stood for all the attractions of life outside the monastery, and St Edmund took him in his arms because he wanted him to become a monk of his church.'

The attractions of the outside world won—until Samson was thirty-one. Only then did he take his vows of obedience as a monk. In those years his strong character developed. His father died while he was a boy. A schoolmaster, William of Diss (a little town on the Norfolk-Suffolk border), gave him his schooling. When he became abbot of Bury, Samson repaid this kindness by finding a good church for William's parson son. Some of Samson's family were well off but they did not help him when he was a poor student. He made a point of not doing any favours for them when, as abbot, he became one of the leading churchmen of England.

There were hardly any students at Oxford yet, but in Paris Peter Abelard's teaching was already famous. Samson went there to study. During his time in Paris, he was kept by a certain chaplain out of profits from the sale of 'Holy Water'. When he became abbot, he sent for that same chaplain and gave him a good church-living too. This picture shows a famous teacher at Paris called Amaury de Bène, with four students. He was about Jocelin's age, and so too young to have taught Samson. Most monks were suspicious of Peter Abelard's teaching and ideas. Even Jocelin became nervous when Samson used to repeat things he had learnt in Paris.

About 1160, Samson obtained the post of *Master of the Scholars,* or *Schoolmaster,* at Bury. Almost at once, the monks appointed him to go to the pope in Rome for a document stating the abbey's rights over a church near Bury. He got the document, but the pope's enemies seized him. He escaped with the document but had to beg his way home. He remembered his dream—at last St Edmund won. He became a monk then, later, abbot:

This drawing from the book by the Bury monk John Lydgate shows the devil's daughter spreading traps to trip up a monk going on a pilgrimage.

'He was of medium height, and very bald. His face was neither round nor long. He had a prominent nose, thick lips, and eyes as clear as glass, seeing everything. His ears too were very sharp. His eyebrows grew shaggy, and he clipped them. A slight cold soon made him hoarse. On the day of his election he was 47, and he had been a monk 17 years. He had a few white hairs in a red beard, and in the hair of his head which had been dark and curly; fourteen years later he was as white as snow.

He preferred fresh milk and honey, and such things, to any other food. He disliked people who grumbled at their food and drink, especially if they were monks; and he kept to his old way of life, as if he was still an ordinary cloister-monk. He could read aloud the Scriptures in English beautifully. He used to preach to the people in English, but in the dialect of his native Norfolk.'

Samson made a clean break with the past twenty years of bungling and borrowing by Abbot Hugh. The moment he arrived back from the king's palace at Bishops Waltham, he showed that he meant to make a complete change in the way the abbey was governed.

Because he knew it would have a dramatic effect, he managed to return to Bury and his abbey on Palm Sunday.

'That morning, when we left the chapter-house, we went out in solemn procession to meet him at the great gate-tower, while from the choir and outside all the bells rang. The great crowds of people outside made it hard for him to move, but as soon as he saw us he got down from his horse, just outside the gate, and after having his boots removed, he was brought barefoot inside the gate, with the prior and sacrist, one on either side.'

First, Samson went to lie at full-length before the high altar, then to the abbot's seat in the monks' choir 'where each of us kissed him in turn', then to the chapter-house 'to thank us for electing him, and to talk to the lawyers and knights who had come to advise him about the government of the surrounding lands'. These lands were what we nowadays call a county or shire. The sheriff (which means shire-reeve, or shire-official) promised Samson they would all help him.

'From there, we went back into the church, to the first Mass. After that, Samson, still barefoot, went to his official residence, to celebrate this day. More than a thousand people ate with him there, amid great rejoicing.'

The very next day, he called in the prior and a few others, as though he was asking their advice—but his plans were already made. He would start by sealing all his official letters and documents with a completely new kind of seal, quite different from the old one Abbot Hugh had used. You can see the new seal on the right. At once the abbey's lawyers and soldiers, and those officials who were not monks, began to say how vain and proud this new abbot was: the old seal, they said, was not good enough for him. They could not see that he had to make this complete break with the past. The most powerful local men, the great land-holders of the neighbourhood, began to learn that this new abbot was able to act on his own. He was not going to talk over his business with them. 'I will be my own steward,' he said. They did not like the sound of that.

Right: *Fifteenth-century Bury drawing of stag-hunt in palisaded park.*
Below: *This barn is one of two at Cressing, in Essex, that go back very nearly to Samson's day.*

He began to have a great list made of all the abbey's farms and the rents and duties that the farmers owed to the abbey. Many years earlier, the king had given the abbey the right to collect a good deal of money that really belonged to him. Previous abbots had not kept accounts of all this. Samson made lists of it all

'. . . even down to the last pennyworth. . . . He called these lists his *Kalendar,* and he used them nearly every day. By looking at them, he could see how good a manager he was, as if he were looking into a mirror. He discovered that, altogether, the abbey was in debt by £3052 3s. 4d. It took twelve years, but he paid off that huge debt.

He remodelled old halls and broken-down houses, through which the crows glided; he built new chapels, and new houses with inner rooms and upper storeys, in several places where there had been no buildings at all, except barns. He also made several parks, and filled them with deer and kept huntsmen and hounds. When he had some grand guest to entertain, he would sometimes sit with his monks in a woodland glade and watch the hounds at the chase, but I never saw him eat venison. He also cleared much woodland, turning it into fields.

He saw to everything himself: as we read in other books, "Caesar did and was everything". He never wasted a moment. Before all else, he saw to the building of barns and cattle-sheds. He kept close watch on the felling and cultivation of his woods. Only one manor was left in the hands of its farmer, an Englishman who was more interested in his farming than in practising French upper-class manners.'

He bought stone houses in Bury and gave them to the Master of the Scholars, so that poor students should not have to pay for lodgings. (Later, he even provided extra funds for the Master, so that students need pay him nothing for their education.) He also built some stone houses in the town. This picture shows Moyses Hall, the most complete stone house surviving in Bury from Samson's day and now a museum.

For fifteen years Samson looked after his abbey well, as well as the king—and indeed the monks— could have wished. By 1198, however, things were turning sour; Samson seemed to be too powerful, doing things that no abbot before had done. Jocelin was worried enough to pick up his quill and begin writing his *Chronicle.* Yet fifteen years is a long time: we can say that the election *had* picked out the right man.

8. Jocelin's story: quarrels and the rule of obedience

To think about

1. Think of two reasons why the abbot might have taken Ralph's side in the argument about wages. Clues: (a) think of the job that Ralph did at the abbey (b) think of the abbot's responsibility to see that his monks were obedient.

To find out

2. Forty knights living on the abbey's estates had to do 'castle-ward' duties at Norwich (page 46). This is an example of 'feudalism' in Jocelin's day. Can you find out more about how feudalism worked?

3. Look at a map (the 1:50 000 Ordnance Survey Map would be best if you can get it) and find Stanford, north of Thetford in Norfolk; it was one of the five places the king appointed for holding tournaments. Look up an atlas and find all the places mentioned in this chapter.

To do

4. Make up and act scenes about (a) Samson's visit to King Richard in prison (b) the officials who dared not take the gold and jewels from St Edmund's shrine (c) the knights who behaved so badly when they came to Bury after the tournament.

5. Draw, or make a cut-out model of, the crusader's badge, a red cross on a white background. Which organisation still uses this symbol?

6. Make models of the abbey buildings at Bury, using your plan and the pictures in this book to help you. Try to make them up into a model of the whole abbey.

Old King Henry II died in 1189 and his elder son, Richard the Lionheart, became king. You can see two of his seals on the left. Richard ruled for ten years but spent only six months of that time in England. His first thought was to go off with a great army to rescue from the Saracens the Holy City of Jerusalem, where Christ was crucified. These expeditions were called 'crusades', which means 'wars of the cross'. Richard twice came within sight of the walls of Jerusalem but was not strong enough to rescue it. On his way home he was shipwrecked, captured and held to ransom in Germany.

The pictures on the left and right show Master Hugo's idea of an attack on Jerusalem as the Prophet Jeremiah described it in the Bible. Hugo painted them for the Bury Bible over fifty years before King Richard's crusade. On 20 November 1190, just before leaving England on the crusade, the king visited Bury to celebrate the anniversary of St Edmund's death. The king was busy raising money to pay for the crusade and Abbot Samson pleased him by paying him the great sum of 1000 marks (a mark was 66 new pence) for a large manor near Bury. Samson did well by his bargain, because that manor brought the abbey £100 yearly in rent. How different from the debt and muddle of Abbot Hugh's time.

When King Richard was captured, his brother John stirred up trouble in England, trying to get control of the kingdom. Samson and all the monks of St Edmund solemnly 'excommunicated' (cut off from the church) these trouble-makers, 'fearing not earl John, the king's brother, nor anybody else'. Then the abbot himself went to Germany to visit Richard in captivity, 'bringing him many gifts'. John remembered this.

Enormous sums of money were needed to pay the king's ransom. Jocelin says everyone all over England had to give all their treasure, but the abbey managed to keep the priceless gold and jewels on St Edmund's shrine. The men at the Royal Exchequer trembled at the thought of stripping St Edmund's shrine:

'Each one of them said "I won't go near it, nor will I. St Edmund's fury can smite people far away, let alone someone who comes close enough to try to remove his shirt." '

In 1194 King Richard was released and he returned briefly to England, where he made five places available for knights to hold tournaments. These had been forbidden up to that time. One place was the heath at Stanford 32 kilometres north of Bury St Edmunds. (It is a battle-training area for the army today.) After one of the tournaments

' eighty young noblemen, fully armed, came to look for lodgings in Bury. The abbot was furious, but tried to keep them quietly in the abbey. He gave them their dinner, and retired to his own rooms for the afternoon. They all started to dance about and sing, and sent into the town for wine. Then they got drunk, and shouted, and did all they could to mock the abbot and make a fool of him in the eyes of the town. Finally, in the evening, they forced their way out of the gates of the abbey and the town.'

Norwich castle

The head of the effigy of King John at Worcester Cathedral.

As Richard had left England again and was fighting against the king of France, all that Samson could do, with the archbishop of Canterbury's help, was to 'excommunicate' these eighty badly-behaved knights. Excommunication frightened many of them. It meant, among other things, that they might go to hell when they died. This illustration from a book in the abbey library shows how they returned to Bury. They stripped themselves almost naked before St Edmund's shrine and offered to wear their chain-mail uniform in his service.

King Richard was certainly in need of that service in Normandy, where, in 1197, he was very hard-pressed. He ordered that one knight out of every ten in England should join him abroad. St Edmund's abbey had always had to support forty knights for 'home defence' duties at Norwich castle. This duty was called 'castle-ward' and it went with the ownership of a certain amount of land. As an important landholder, the abbot normally expected to have to keep the forty knights at Norwich for forty days each year. Now Richard was hoping to get one in ten of all his knights to serve abroad all year.

The Bury knights told Samson they did not owe that kind of service: neither they nor their forefathers had ever served abroad, they said. The worried abbot crossed to Normandy to consult the king. Richard said he did not want money—he must have the four knights (one-tenth of forty). Samson saw that he must hire four and pay them himself for their expenses. They reported for duty at a place called Eu on the coast of Normandy.

King Richard made good use of his soldiers. In 1199 he reached an agreement with the French king. Then, outside a small castle, in a fight not connected with the war at all, he was hit in the shoulder by an arrow and died. That was a bad day for Samson. Do you remember how he had supported King Richard against his brother John? John now became king.

After his coronation John went straight to Bury, where he was richly looked after. Jocelin complains that 'he offered nothing to the Saint in return save 12 pence sterling'. It is not very surprising, is it?

Jocelin had by now become cellarer, second only to the prior who came next under the abbot. It was a hard job, and Jocelin's feelings are clear when he describes the affair of Ralph the porter who was responsible for seeing who went into and out of the abbey through the great Norman gate-tower.

Ralph had upset the senior abbey officials, Jocelin's colleagues: although a servant, he had given evidence against them in the law-courts. They reduced his wages. He complained to the abbot. The officials stood firm. The abbot was angry. He publicly ordered the cellarer (Jocelin) to restore Ralph to his full salary and to drink nothing but water till then. Jocelin chose to drink water for one day. Next day the abbot forbade him both meat and drink until he had obeyed. The abbot then wisely went away for eight days. Jocelin says, 'there was a great uproar in the monastery, such as I never saw before, and they said that the abbot's order ought not to be obeyed'. But of course it was, and 'we humbled ourselves before him. Seeing that we were overcome, he was himself overcome.' Ralph kept his full wages.

We reach the last episode in Jocelin's *Chronicle*, in 1201 or 1202, when Samson was sixty-six or sixty-seven. His health was failing. King John sent for him, to discuss some orders sent by the pope. Samson knew that, whatever he said, he would offend either king or pope.

'He actually asked our advice, a thing he had hardly ever done before. Coming into the chapter-house on the day before his departure, he had all his own books brought in with him and he made a present of them to our church and library. At this moment, three monks of very little sense started to say that the abbot had always looked after his own rights as abbot. Would he, before he went off to see the king, make sure that the monks were not weakened as a result of the abbot's great rights? When he heard this, he said things that should not be said, swearing that he would be obeyed as long as he lived. Then he calmed down . . . and promised that, when he returned, he would always work with our advice and would restore to everyone whatever was his just right.' A certain calm was restored but, 'as Ovid wrote, "anyone can give away promises".'

Those are the *Chronicle*'s last words. In John's reign, all the barons of England grew more concerned, like the Bury monks, about rights and promises. In 1215, this led to the signing of the Great Charter, *Magna Carta*, at Runnymede. Abbot Samson had died four years previously but perhaps Jocelin lived to see it.

The graves in the chapter-house in the ruins of Bury abbey. Samson's grave is second from the front.

Acknowledgments

We are grateful to the following for their kind assistance in providing illustrations.

Aerofilms Ltd for pages 3, 33, 46
Alinari for page 28
Auguste Allemand for page 39
Bodleian Library for pages 22, 27, 34
Cambridge University Collection, copyright reserved, for page 29
Cambridge University Library for pages 14, 19, 23
Crown-copyright records in the Public Record Office, by permission of the Controller of
  H.M. Stationery Office, page 36
Europa Verlag A.G., Zurich for page 16
Gabinetto Fotografico della soprintendenza alle Gallerie di Firenze for page 28
Hodder and Stoughton Ltd for page 2
A F Kersting for pages 11, 13, 15, 21, 30, 31, 37, 40, 46
Lambeth Palace Library for page 31
Master and Fellows of Corpus Christi College, Cambridge for pages 20, 21, 22, 44, 45
Master and Fellows of Trinity College, Cambridge for page 22
Metropolitan Museum of Art, The Cloisters Collection, Purchase 1963 for pages 18, 19
Michael Nicholson for page 43
National Monuments Record for pages 15, 25, 37, 38, 47
The late Edwin Smith and Mrs Olive Smith for pages 17, 42
The Suffolk Institute of Archaeology for page 7
Trustees of the British Museum for pages 4, 6, 7, 8, 10, 24, 26, 27, 28, 41, 42, 43, 44, 45, 46
The Warburg Institute for pages 39, 44
Plan on page 12 based on plans by A B Whittingham (HMSO official guide to Bury St
  Edmunds Abbey) and by R Gilyard-Beer (Proceedings of the Suffolk Institute of
  Archaeology).
Plan on page 32 based on plans by A B Whittingham (Archaeological Journal, 1952;
  HMSO guide 1971).

Bibliography

Some books to read

J Sayers, *Life in a Medieval Monastery* (Focus on History Series, Longman Group, 1969)
M Reeves, *The Medieval Monastery* (Then and There Series, Longman Group)
R J Unstead, *Monasteries* (A & C Black, 1970)
J Langdon-Davies (ed.), *Henry VIII and Dissolution of the Monasteries* (Jackdaw Publications, 1966)
D Macaulay, *Cathedral* (Collins, 1974)

More difficult books

The most convenient text of Jocelin's *Chronicle* is H E Butler's edition (Nelson's Medieval classics, 1949), with the Latin original and English translation on facing pages. Its introduction is seriously out of date, especially since R H C Davis edited Abbot Samson's *Kalendar* for the Camden Society (1954), showing for the first time that Jocelin held the high office of cellarer in the abbey. Two other works have provided the basis for this book: M R James's *On the Abbey of St Edmund at Bury* (Cambridge, 1895), and A B Whittingham's official guide-book to Bury St Edmunds Abbey, published for the Department of the Environment (HMSO, 1971). Davis's evidence has been recently, but erroneously, questioned.

E Smith and O Cook, *English Abbeys and Priories* (Thames and Hudson, 1960)
J Evans (ed.), *The Flowering of the Middle Ages* (see Chapter 2, *The Monastic World*, Thames and Hudson, 1966)
A L Poole, *From Domesday Book to Magna Carta, 1087-1216* (Oxford University Press, 1955)
Dom D Knowles, *The Religious Orders in England* (3 vols., Cambridge University Press, 1948-59)
Dom D Knowles and R N Hadcock, *Medieval Religious Houses in England and Wales* (a very full catalogue of all known religious houses, Longman Group, 1971)